FULFILMENT IN YOUR CREATION

YOUR ACCOMPLISHMENTS ARE ENTIRELY YOUR OWN

DR. (COL) SHAJI PANIKKAR

ISBN 979-8-89026-717-7

CONTENTS

Chapter - 1

DEFINE LIFE

If you believe in and respect the four words **Matha, Pitha, Guru, and Daivam (mother, father, teacher, and god)**, you will be a good human being, a blessed person, and a good citizen not only in your lifetime but also for future generations.

"----A mother, LOVE her, RESPECT her----"

-----Mother, those six simple words mean the world to us. Everything that hurts in the world weighs heavily on the shoulders of one woman. Making room for you. Having her approval is an invaluable present. Pay her the-----

-----A child's power lies in those six letters, Father. Fathers provide not only material but also psychological and social security. He has been through so much and is in so much pain, but he has no one to talk to about it. Honour and cherish your dad. He will be your pillar of support.-----

------When it comes to influencing a child's development, no one is more influential than a child's teacher. Educators serve as examples to their students in many ways. They mould students into successful adults. Teachers are viewed as the foundation upon which the next generation will be built.-------

"RESPECT your teachers."

----We exist because GOD made us, and GOD continues to care for us. As human beings, we ought to accept God's gifts and worship him. Your efforts will pay off.----

Your goal is to live a happy life. You will undoubtedly succeed. If you want to live a happy life, you must work hard in a variety of ways. You worked hard, and you will be rewarded for it. But what exactly is life? In any case, everyone tries to explain life. Everyone understands that the journey is more important than the destination, and that it will lead us to it. Success and failure, happiness and unhappiness, enjoyment and struggle, peace and worry, health and wealth, liabilities and debts, and so on are all part of our lives. What causes these occurrences, and who is the perpetrator? Why is it that a wealthy man is occasionally seen standing in the rain or eating in a local Dhaba? In that situation, he must be having a good time. That is the way life is. Make sure that whatever you do for your own pleasure and happiness does not hurt or harm the feelings of others.

Everything is determined by what you create in your life. God created you, and you must forge your own path in life. You are each in charge of shaping your own life. Can anyone, on the other hand, define life? Nobody can, in my opinion, define it. Carol Edith Cleland, an American philosopher, debated the lack of a definition of life with many scientists. She stated emphatically, "Life is different." It cannot be defined simply by linking concepts. As a result, looking for a laundry list of traits that will prove to be the true definition of life is pointless. "What we really want to know is what life is, not what we think the word means to us." And, according to Cleland, we must abandon our search for a definition in order to satisfy our desire.

Do you want to create a happy family, a good society, and a wonderful country? I'm sure we all want it, but how many of us are willing to put in the effort to achieve it and live a happy life? Do you want to be the personification of your life?

The act of living is defined as life, and it can take many different forms. Nobody will remember it or understand the precise value of the time we have between birth and death. As we go about our daily lives, we are aware that death has been a part of our lives since birth. We all come into this world crying, and for many, that cry brings joy. Many people will celebrate by throwing parties, handing out candy, and participating in various other activities. We learn a lot as we get older and start doing things for ourselves in order to be successful. Then, as we progress through life, we do a variety of good and bad things, with almost everyone exhibiting possessiveness and selfishness in amassing numerous assets, name and fame, and so on. However, after experiencing everything and accumulating all assets while ignoring everyone else's worries and struggles, we will leave this world with only a few people crying.

After a few days, the name, fame, and all relationships, among other things, will fade away. Tears will become more common over time. Life unfolds in a cyclical pattern. It will affect everyone at some point; the only question is when and where. Throughout our lives, however, we are all driven to succeed. We accept responsibilities at various stages of our lives, sometimes as a challenge. Life is lovely and valuable, but we must first learn to appreciate it.

Life is precious and beautiful, but we must first love ourselves before embarking on a wonderful journey through life. If you love yourself, you will take care of yourself, be happy, and maintain your mental and physical health. "If you truly loved yourself, you could never hurt another," said Buddha. Life is meaningful when we have a goal. According to Aristotle, the purpose and ultimate goal of life is to achieve eudaimonia ('happiness'). He considered eudaimonia to be more than just virtue or pleasure, but rather the practise of virtue. Everyone wants to live a happy life, but how many actually do? Everyone can amass enormous wealth, name, and fame, but there is no life without happiness. Everything is changing as a result of our attitude. How can you sustain your happiness when you have ego, arrogance, dishonesty, envy, hatred, immorality, lying, greed, violence, unreliability, selfishness, and so on?

I will emphasise the importance of growth, contribution, connections, creativity, value, respect, love, support, peace, and so on. We are all blessed to be born as humans. Animals and birds have lives, too. However, it cannot be compared to human life. Humans have an excellent brain that enables them to think and act.

Our lives, and how you lead them, will be based on your artistic way of living, understanding and balancing situations, giving value in all aspects, and updating knowledge, as life is a circle that rotates in 360 degrees. When you are born as a baby and gradually begin to grow, reaching various stages without knowing anything, In the meantime, you start learning new things and developing a better understanding of situations. Everyone will unconditionally love, care for, and protect you as a child. It has the backing of parents. Your parents, on the other hand, must be concerned in order to provide you with comfort, safety, and security, and a child will be unaware of the difficulties. Everything is normal in your own world when you are a child and have no worries.

Anyone, young or old, must understand and manage the situation. As you develop, so will your ability to comprehend and analyse the world around you. In general, you take situations lightly and assume that everything is fine. Things are not to be taken lightly. Every moment and every situation is significant and should be treated as such.

Bhagwan Krishna discussed sin and the significance of good karma. Taking responsibility for one's life, living up to one's potential, and broadening one's experience envelope is how to earn good karma; sitting on the sidelines, doing nothing, refusing to take responsibility, and expecting riches to fall on you is a sure way to incur sin because life is a learning experience.

Everyone on the planet has an idealised vision of how their life should be. But is it easy to make the dream a reality? There are numerous stumbling blocks to overcome in everyday life. If we begin to examine each stage of our lives, we can conclude that we can live a good life regardless of the difficulties we face. It is critical that you conduct research on the success formula and be adaptable in order to make our lives happy. Everything is entirely under our control. We are all here on this planet and have no idea what our lives are worth. Doing something and being content with the small outcome of your efforts. In my opinion, at each stage of our important lives, we should begin thoroughly analysing situations.

We are all aware that there are different stages of life, such as birth, education, employment, marriage, childbirth and development, and finally retirement. It may begin counting at any time. We enter a new phase of our lives and embark on an entirely new journey when we marry. Our responsibilities have grown, we need to think in order to grow, and we will start planning for the future. A large number of people will begin to make a difference.

A newlywed couple is in a different world with different emotions. Both will forget everything and start living a new life full of new experiences. They may be unable to separate for an hour. Love will fall like rain.

When we speak or think about life, we tend to focus on our own happiness, growth, accomplishments, accumulating wealth, popularity, and so on. How many of us think about our nature, society, and country, to name a few things? All of these factors, in addition to your own, must be considered. Nobody should become selfish in this world. Many poor people around you must be starving for a single meal of any variety or quality. According to 2019–2021 data, approximately 16.4 percent of India's population is poor, with 4.2 percent living in extreme poverty because their deprivation score is greater than 50%. Around 18.7 percent of the population is vulnerable and is likely to be pushed to the brink of disaster.

When someone is in deep grief, how can they sleep peacefully and soundly? I have a vision of a beautiful life full of values that not only develop individuals but also our nation as a whole. "If a country is to be corrupt-free and become a nation of beautiful minds, I strongly believe there are three key societal members who can make a difference," says Dr. APJ Abdul Kalam. "They are the father, mother, and teacher." As a result, parents and teachers bear primary responsibility for the development of the family, society, and nation. With all amenities and facilities available all around, our generation has forgotten to create a beautiful life, instead damaging the nation with the quickest move of new culture and thought process. Who will be held accountable for the harm that is being done in the family, society, and nation?

If you want to live a happy life, you should include any contributions you have made to the development of your family, society, and nation. You must be settling down at home. You should not, however, become happy as a result of this. One of your responsibilities is to build a nation. To that end, all parents should pledge that they will properly educate their children, and that their growth will undoubtedly help to advance your society and the nation as a whole.

It must be obvious that parents must now make every effort to support their children, despite the numerous challenges they face. Parents, on the other hand, are becoming powerless as a result of children's culture. Every moment we create, whether it is happiness, sorrow, enjoyment in any form, struggle, and so on, It is entirely up to you to live in a happy, loving, and respectful family. Respect for one another is essential in a family and in life, especially for elders and parents. Nobody can assist you in creating a good family from the outside. Because of how teenagers behave at home, most families miss out on all of this. There is no consideration, love, or respect for one another.

It's incredible to think back on the carefree days of my youth and see how happy everyone was. Everyone treated each other with kindness, compassion, and dignity. These days, most things are obsolete because of technological progress. We've given up on letters and messages in favour of texting and instant messaging; we've given up on face-to-face contact in favour of video chats; we've given up on torches in favour of mobile phone lights; we've given up on photo studios in favour of smartphones; we've given up on reading newspapers in favour of a mobile phone app called "daily hunt"; we've given up on going to the movies in favour of watching them on our phones; and we' We don't send our kids to tutors, and they use mobile apps for their studies. When we used to listen to music on the radio, we now use our phones; when we used to go to the bank, we would have to wait in line; when we wanted to see a movie, we would have to go to a movie theatre; when we wanted to check our spelling, we would have to buy a dictionary, but now we just use our phones; when we wanted to eat out, we would go to a restaurant, but now we use mobile apps to place our orders.

The advent of mobile phones, a single instrument, has grasped our lives and ushered in a new era for everyone. There have been many gains and losses throughout our lives.

New technologies appear every day, but are we also expanding our minds at the same rate? Nobody gets anywhere in life unless they work on themselves intellectually. The time has come for us to hone our intellect and evolve into a selfless, obedient humanistic way of life. If we put forth the effort, we can all improve ourselves and the world around us.

Chapter - 2

THE BIRTH OF THE CHILD

All of your priorities and attention will shift the moment your child is born. The mother of the child will be unable to care for her husband. Both husband and wife will be unable to spend time together, and the action will change frequently throughout. The husband and wife must make significant mental and physical sacrifices in their family life. They've just started a new life together, a union of two minds, two feelings, and two dreams. They are more concerned with the child. They are prepared to face it and will do so for the rest of their lives. Regardless of whether they become father and mother, grandfather or grandmother, their children are always children to them. However, they will not feel bad or lonely because the new bone child is the priority, and the baby is the game changer and focal point. Ignoring their own lives and enjoyment, the entire focus would be on the child's development and upbringing by meeting all of the child's needs.

----Every child is a blessing from God with the potential to reach his or her fullest potential. However, growth is situationally dependent. In a perfect world, everyone would be perfect.----

They are prepared to make any sacrifice for the sake of the child. The conflict will not be resolved in a few years but rather over a quarter-century or more. They will live a different life now that they have a child. This change comes with a lot of responsibility. They will both start thinking about the child and his or her future. They, as parents, begin to consider schooling their child and relocating based on the availability of the best school and college, and so on. They also plan their finances and save for the child. If the parents are focused and forward-thinking, they will start laying the groundwork for their child's education, job placement, marriage, and overall setup before the child reaches the age of formal schooling. As a result, they begin to work towards their objective.

A new life awaits them, and all of their attention will be focused on the child. They will not have time to consider them because they will be preoccupied with the child. They are prepared to make a sacrifice for the sake of the child. Their sole goal would be to properly raise the child. The child, on the other hand, will be unaware of all of these facts and will never fully comprehend them in his or her lifetime. Even the parents will not tell their children about their sacrifice.

Caring for a child can last for days, weeks, months, or years. They or the child will be unaware of the child's growth. Without realising it, the child will grow, and the parent will age by focusing on studies and counting their children's grades in schools and colleges. Their emotions and even their energy levels will change dramatically. In fact, they will be concerned about the child's reaction as she or he grows while doing everything for the child.

As the child grows, the parent begins to focus on instilling in the child's mind the values and ethics necessary to become a good human being. When children are young, they understand and listen to their parents. However, as they enter adolescence, they begin to disregard all values and ethics, as well as any good things they learned from their parents or teachers, and they even mock all of these, as well as the efforts of their parents and teachers. In this case, society frequently blames parents for their children's inhuman behaviour.

They are, however, completely innocent because they made every effort. The parent should work hard to raise their child to be a good human being and citizen of the country. Parents should not expect their child to be obedient if they are not focused on doing this and neglect all of these important things. In this case, the parent is ambitious and has a good plan for the child's development. Certain areas, however, will be ignored. Along with the parent's efforts, the child's development should be taken into account. The child should start small and enjoy doing them on his or her own. Parenting entails not only giving birth to a child, but also caring for the child, putting in a lot of effort and suffering to raise and educate the child. On the other hand, due to their busy or mechanical lives, most parents fail to properly educate their children at home.

The first school for a child is his or her own home. The child should not be blamed later if the parent does not provide opportunities for the child to learn and grow. Parental overindulgence and failure to task the child in the hope that the child will be happy and receive love for the rest of their life. Parents have unrealistically high expectations. Unless the child learns from the ground up, he or she will learn nothing and will be unable to face future life challenges.

A child should be given responsibility for his or her own actions from an early age. As a result, the child will become more responsible, bold, and prepared to face any challenges. Such a child will almost certainly grow up to be extremely sharp, bright, and intelligent. People are praying for and having children. That parent is happy and considers himself or herself fortunate. However, they are not considering their responsibility to raise the child in the most effective way possible in order to produce a good human being and citizen. If everyone works hard to ensure that not only our country, but the entire world, will be perfect in the next two generations, To teach a child the value of life, the parent should start teaching the child from the beginning. If it starts at the beginning, it will help the child learn to value everything. It will be ineffective if it occurs later in the process. Because the child's mind and development are at a different stage by then, and he or she may not value new experiences. The child should learn everything practically.

Since the child begins to crawl and sit, he or she should encourage himself or herself to eat. Generally, the child will be carried in the arm while being fed stories and shown various objects. In that case, we are undermining the bravery of the child. Animals and birds must be observed and studied. Animals and birds are quickly becoming self-sufficient. It takes humans many decades to achieve independence. Some mothers are also raising a child who will attend college. It is not love or affection, but rather spoiling and weakening the child, and such a child will not succeed in life. Such a child will always be dependent, and if they are not, they will fail in life.

Parents should instil responsibility in their children at a young age. Whether they come from a wealthy or impoverished family, they instil responsibility in their children. Whether they come from a wealthy or impoverished family. The child should be encouraged to prepare his or her schoolbag for the following day according to the schedule and should be allowed to carry it throughout. Because of their parents' excessive pampering, children are not allowed to do many tasks that they are expected to do. Many parents assist their children in packing their school bags in accordance with the schedule. Parents should insist on their children doing the same, initially under their supervision. In that case, the child will quickly learn to be responsible and perfect.

Assigning the child various small tasks, such as keeping their own belongings, such as books, play materials, etc., in proper places, assisting the mother with various household tasks, cleaning his or her room, and encouraging the child to do small things, is critical. When we give them minor tasks, we should be patient enough to provide corrections and encouragement. Because the father may not always be available, the mother is the best person to shape the child. If both parents work and the child is placed in creche, for example, the child will lack self-esteem. Children must spend time with their parents or grandparents.

All tasks, no matter how small or large, should be appreciated and shared by the parent. Recognize the child for even minor accomplishments such as drawing a picture, eating food as directed by the mother, or whatever else they attempted. These kinds of compliments will boost courage and motivation. In addition, the child will come out of fear of what he has to do on a daily basis. Making the child courageous will assist the child in overcoming his or her fear and becoming more confident in life.

Many children in our society are not properly guided by their parents because both parents work and must focus on their jobs. Their top priorities are their job, salary, and advancement. They cannot survive unless they work. How can they focus on development in this situation? It is critical for their survival that they work. Raising a good citizen or a future leader is equally important. A child will not become anything unless his or her parents accept responsibility for him or her. Even with great effort, today's children are not becoming obedient. Parents must focus on their child's proper development; in this case, the current system will change over time, and all children will begin to be disciplined. Whatever they see and experience now will stick with them for the rest of their lives because it has been recorded in their minds. It is irreversible and will be passed down from generation to generation.

We have first-hand knowledge or examples from the past. A few decades ago, women were either not allowed to work or were not preferred to work. The ladies were only at home, which helped children develop properly. The joint family and the culture of the time cannot be compared. As a result, future generations will miss out on a lot.

In general, even if a mother is always available at home, she may not assign a task to her child because she believes it will be too much for her. She will not believe that such tasks will help the child's mental development. The mother's sole focus should be the child's development. Many mothers are unaware of the significance of proper child development. They must be well educated, but either do not understand or are unconcerned about the fundamentals of parenting. Many mothers and fathers yell at their children for insignificant reasons, and such children will not develop normally. Parental attention and dedication are critical for the proper development of the child, both mentally and physically.

A small child, with a small and innocent mind, becomes happy in the micro-level reactions of either parents, relatives, or anyone else who happens to be present around the child at the time. A child has no relatives, and no one who is holding him or her is close to the child. The child will gravitate towards whoever is playing with or making the child laugh. What we should take from this is that the innocent mind of a child prefers only happiness. Anyone, including raising your voice, should not harm a child. The small mind expects only love and affection. A small child has been shown to recognise the person who makes him or her happy and safe. At this stage, mental development is critical, and parents can only assist their children.

We've all noticed that when new people, whether guests or relatives, visit our homes, small children behave differently in order to gain the attention and approval of others. Family members do not appear to be taking care of such situations, and the child appears to be waiting for someone to come and recognise the child's talent. We are all aware of this, but are we making an effort to review and correct the situation for the sake of the child's happiness? A child requires undivided attention, which we must provide as parents; otherwise, the child will not grow properly.

We buy various items for the child, such as puzzles and other playing tools, but once the child begins to play, they are generally not allowed to play and are directed to read a book. The child's mind will be completely focused on the playing tools in this case, and he or she will be unable to concentrate on his or her studies. The child must physically be sitting with the book, but the parent will be pleased and think, "My child is very good and has obeyed and is doing his or her studies." But what will be the outcome? Without a doubt, the child did not study at all. This child is unhappy; he squandered valuable time; and he was unable to study. Because his mind was on the puzzle, the child must complete all of his or her own tasks.

Parents should instil in their children the importance of self-sufficiency in all aspects of their lives. It is critical to instil the value of everything in them. The child should understand how things work and the significance of everything. In reality, a child should understand life's difficulties. It is important to provide comforts, but the child must value everything. At a young age, a child should be exposed to reality and difficulties. A child of this calibre will undoubtedly grow up to be perfect and responsible. The child should be given decision-making authority.

A child should be given the opportunity to choose their own things since childhood. For example, if you are buying a dress for a child, you should allow the child to choose the colour. If a disadvantage exists, the child will consider how to correct it. The child will gain confidence and courage. Even 2- and 3-year-olds can now select their favourite colour of clothing and play materials. However, the parent has his or her own preferences and will not allow the child to choose accordingly. In such cases, the parents win, but in the long run, the parents lose because their child's mind does not develop properly, which will irritate the parent. We should give the child the authority to choose and satisfy themselves. So it is solely the responsibility of the parent to give birth, raise the child with complete confidence and courage, instil a value system in them, and raise a good human being and citizen. It is a massive task that must not be underestimated; otherwise, we will cause significant damage.

I've seen several instances where a child is crying in public, such as at a shopping mall or a sweet shop, and the parent is beating or pinching the child to get the child to stop crying. Most of the time, the child is crying because he or she requires something that the parent has refused to provide. In such cases, the parent should provide whatever minor items the child requests or demands in order to provide the child with satisfaction and happiness. The parent should be aware of their child's emotions. Everything cannot be denied. Provide the item and teach the child in a systematic manner while avoiding any harm to the child. It is critical to comprehend the child's small mind.

Childhood is a critical stage, according to psychologist Debosree Bhattacharjee. A bad childhood can also have a negative impact on an individual's adulthood. As a result, understanding your child's personality is an essential part of parenting. Only by getting to know your child well will you be able to focus on his talents and positive characteristics, giving him a well-rounded personality in the years to come. As a parent, you should pay attention to your child's development outside of school, taking into account their interests and passions. If a child wishes, he or she should be permitted to practise or learn music. Everything has its time and place. If a child begins and continues to practise music, he or she will become a professional in the field. Almost every child will get off to a good start, but only a few will make it all the way to the end. The majority of the children will abandon the art and later bemoan the fact that they did not continue and thus missed out on an excellent opportunity. Based on your age and experience, you should take command of the situation.

I am confident that if every child is motivated and supported well at the right time by parents and teachers, our society will produce a large number of talented and disciplined children. Any child who participates in extracurricular activities will have a different focus, and such a child will develop into a well-disciplined and progressive individual. If parents are only concerned with their child's grades, there is a good chance that the child will underperform and become bored, which will eventually lead to the child developing unwanted habits and neglecting the progressive life.

Beyond academics, parents must educate themselves in order to support their children's development. Every child, at the appropriate age, should be given the opportunity to participate in a variety of activities in addition to academics. This will result in the child's mental and physical development being excellent.

If you want your children to be intelligent, read them fairy tales, according to Albert Einstein. Read them more fairy tales if you want them to be smarter. As we all know, children are our future leaders. Our primary responsibility is to prepare them for anything. A child should be able to deal with any difficulties that life throws at them. A child's concern should be for his or her family, society, and country. It will not occur by itself. These lessons must be repeated on a regular basis. They should learn about society, how people struggle for different things, how we can assist such people, why it is important, and so on. If a child sees someone going hungry, he or she should be willing to share his or her food with them. We must become influential by promoting the growth of a good society and nation.

Most parents nowadays are selfish about their children, and the child who understands this will only act in this manner. The child will also become selfish and lack a helpful attitude. A child is capable of quickly learning or comprehending situations. If you create favourable conditions, they will grow and should be beneficial to the family, society, and nation. We make everything ourselves. We are the creators, along with Brahma. If you are the sole creator of your family, society, and nation, why not do it in such a way that others remember you for the rest of their lives? Always look on the bright side. Do it on a regular basis.

Chapter - 3

EDUCATION

When a child starts school, his or her parents have a lot of worries about him or her. Children, on the other hand, do not comprehend anything, including the importance of education. When a child begins school, the experience must be managed in such a way that the child enjoys it. Who will be the source of learning attraction and interest? It is entirely up to the parents, with some help from teachers. We are laying the groundwork for the development of a future leader and a good human being at a critical juncture, so we must take it seriously. The child, with his or her very innocent mind, begins to comprehend what they see and face in their daily activities. If the situation does not favour the child in his or her small mind, the child will almost certainly reject it. In that case, the child will believe that his or her parents are sending him or her to school as part of the process.

As a child grows and advances to the next grade level, he or she begins to value education. The study effort or priority given to learning may not be motivated by the desire to become something but rather by the nature of competition created by the influence of circumstances. Of course, as a parent, you put a lot of pressure on your child to do well in school. Parents would be proud of their children if they received good grades in the eyes of the rest of society. Even at that point, parents have no idea where their child will go or who he or she will become.

You, as a parent, set high expectations for the child without understanding the child, without knowing the child's future, without understanding the importance of education, and even without knowing your own potential. You have created a situation in which you have received no results commensurate with your efforts as a result of your attitude. When a child attends school, he or she gradually updates himself or herself and begins to do things for themselves, understanding the value and importance of education. As a parent, however, you are not allowing your child to think and grow as he or she desires in life. You, as a parent in authority, are ruining the atmosphere because of your preconceived plans and ideas about the child.

I've seen many parents make the same mistakes and feel proud of themselves for putting academic pressure on their children. While focusing solely on grades, they eventually forget many other very important things that are required for the child's growth. When parents compare their child to other children who are receiving higher grades than their own, they become impatient. Comparison will demoralise the child, causing him or her to lose rather than gain ability. Appreciation would energise people of all ages, especially children. As a result, it is critical for the child's proper development that you handle the child with appropriate words or treatment.

Every child is gifted and intelligent, but their circumstances prevent them from reaching their full potential. In their own development, there will always be a controlling force and many barriers. Controlling and denying their needs, as well as failing to listen, will suppress their minds at an early age. If the child's brain development is halted, he or she will not grow. In order for the child's brain and mind to develop, he or she should be given the opportunity to think. It is obvious that nothing will grow unless the brain is used. If parents and elders do not erect barriers, the child may think and begin to develop his or her own potential. They each have their own distinct personality.

Sachin Tendulkar is a prime example. He would have gotten a job if he had studied hard and continued his education. However, he dropped out of school to pursue his passion, and he eventually accomplished everything in his life and became world famous in the field of cricket. A passion should be developed. Don't just limit yourself to studying. This world provides us with numerous opportunities.

Four cognitive theories, according to Jean Piaget, a well-known Swiss psychologist, are extremely beneficial to a child's development. These are the four theories:

Sensorimotor Stage: The period between birth and the age of two years during which an infant's knowledge of the world is limited to sensory perceptions and motor activities. The extent of behaviour is simple motor responses caused by sensory stimuli.

Pre-operational Stage: The time between the ages of two and six when a child begins to learn to use language. Children do not understand concrete logic at this stage, are unable to mentally manipulate information, and are unable to consider the perspectives of others.

Concrete Operational Stage: Ages 7–11, when children begin to understand mental operations. Children start to think logically about concrete events, but they struggle to understand abstract or hypothetical concepts.

The period from the age of 12 to adulthood during which people develop their ability to think abstractly Skills like logical thought, deductive reasoning, and systematic planning emerge during this stage.

The current educational system is ineffective in terms of student development. When we look at the current educational situation, we can see that the child's standard is rapidly deteriorating. In reality, children are not learning enough in schools or colleges under the current educational system. We should certainly appreciate the teachers' efforts. However, as can be seen, the student learned nothing in life. When they start working, the total amount of talent required for the job and life skills varies. How will we bridge the gap? The child's language skills are lacking, as are his or her innovative ideas and practical knowledge.

Many engineering graduates are now employed in the banking sector, which has no connection to the engineering profession. When they start doing bank work, they have a difficult time keeping up. Only extensive bank job and portfolio training will allow them to be adjusted. Professional training is distinct, but so is life experience. A child who has learned life skills since childhood has a greater chance of success in life.

If we closely examine a person's capability, we may discover that he or she is unable to fill out a form, handle a bank transaction, write a check leaf, write an application, and a variety of other micro-level actions. So, how can we say he or she is educated? The reason for their failure in these areas of their lives is that their parents and teachers did not provide them with the opportunity to do so. After graduation, parents are proud of their children's education, but they have learned nothing in life.

All practical knowledge needed in our daily lives must be taught during our education, whether in school or college. Completing a college education implies that a person is capable of dealing with anything and doing everything successfully in their daily lives without the assistance of others. How are we going to do it? We need to change our education system and educate parents on how to avoid overindulging their children and denying them opportunities.

Children should be given opportunities to participate in anything and everything from the time they are born. Living a beautiful life, as I previously stated, is an art. Everyone has the potential to succeed. But how you focus on it, how much you value it, and how you want to take advantage of all available resources depend. Life should be settled by the age of 50, and after that, one should have a very peaceful life. To accomplish this, it must be properly driven. Saving money, accumulating assets for the future, and so on are all important aspects of life. All of this should be learned and practised during the educational process. Despite numerous failure stories, most young people today are preoccupied with their extravagant lifestyles and are unwilling to save for the future. In life, financial planning is essential. Earning money is not an art form, but saving money is. Those who learn to save for a better future will have a better life. Proper education should begin at a young age in order to learn all of these important aspects of life. Many young boys who have recently begun working and earning money plan for various investments, including land. Saving is, of course, necessary and unavoidable for a bright future.

Those with a lot of money and property will be recognised and respected in today's world. Even in our own homes, if you are unable to meet your children's or spouse's day-to-day needs, they may feel guilty and begin comparing themselves to others who meet all of their children's and spouse's needs. As a result, if you are unable to meet the needs of your own family members, you gradually lose respect, love, and affection, even within your own home. To have a bright future and a happy life, one must become passionate about saving and investing and set priorities accordingly. Many world-famous people rose from humble beginnings to become the world's richest person. Consider Warren Buffett, who started out delivering newspapers, selling golf balls, stamps, Coca-Cola, and weekly magazines, among other things. As a teenager, he began investing in the stock market. He is currently the world's fifth-wealthiest person, with a net worth of $ 108 billion. So anyone can develop such habits, but how you want to be is entirely up to you.

Everything is entirely your creation. Small children are required to carry heavy bags containing books that they are unable to carry in today's education system. Children attending college or higher education, on the other hand, have only one or two books, and many are going without any books at all. My recommendation is that students in the lowest grades have no books or only one or two books, and that classes be limited to one or two subjects per day. If we teach in a systematic manner, with a new timetable of one or two subjects per day, the child will be able to easily carry his bag, and the parents will not have to carry it.

Our educational system has changed dramatically and ineffectively in the last few decades for a variety of reasons, several decades. Our old gurukul (guru means teacher and Kul or kula means home) education system was excellent, and many other countries, including Europe, the Middle East, and Portugal, came to India for quality education. Since ancient times, India has had a long tradition of learning and education. Gurukul was both the physical home for teachers, or Acharya, and the centre of learning where students lived until they finished their education. Teachers and students shared a house or lived in close proximity. Children who join the Gurukul will only return home once they have completed their education. There were no fees; only gurudakshina, or respect for the teacher, was collected. It could be in the form of money or any task assigned by the guru or teacher. The goal of such education was to teach students in a natural setting while they shared brotherhood, love, empathy, humanity, and discipline. Language, science, and mathematics were the main subjects taught through group discussions, self-learning, and other methods.

Through the teaching of arts, sports, crafts, and singing, there was also a focus on developing students' critical thinking and intelligence. Aside from these studies, there was yoga, meditation, and other activities. All of this aided in the process of personality development by increasing their confidence, sense of discipline, intellect, and mindfulness, which are all necessary even today to face the world ahead.

In my opinion, we should return to our previous educational system culture, which will help us create very good youth and develop our country well. In today's educational system, children work hard to memorise answers in order to receive a good grade, and grades are the only focus. As a result, when confronted with various situations, the young generation is off track and completely failing. Life skills are critical in today's world, and they are lacking in today's educational system. The teacher-student relationship is also unfathomable, and our educators are struggling to educate our children. To some extent, students today do not regard teachers as necessary as they once did. Those who value teachers will undoubtedly listen to and obey them.

Aside from formal education, we can learn a lot from our surroundings and daily lives. What we learn in our daily lives is the best education. Every day is an education, and those who value it will be respected throughout their lives. When a child starts asking for different materials for school activities, he or she should be taken to the store with someone and then allowed to go and buy what he or she needs. This action will help the child's brain development as well as his or her confidence and courage. But how many parents follow through? These are just a few suggestions for properly developing your child. From an early age, children should be involved in the purchase of household items such as vegetables, milk, and so on.

When parents go shopping, they should bring their children along and teach them about the family's needs as well as selecting and purchasing items from the store. Furthermore, the child should be made aware of the price and payment system. As the child grows older, he or she may be able to go shopping on his or her own. As a result, such activities will undoubtedly improve one's understanding of managing finances and household items. This type of education would be superior to a traditional school or college education and would benefit the child's future development. What is the Bhagavad Gita's take on education? Gita claims that receiving virtual knowledge is the true meaning of education, but the question remains, "What is virtual knowledge?" We know God exists everywhere when we see or feel the universe in all of its diversity. True wisdom teaches us to see God in every soul.

Until the second or third grade, education should be based on physical knowledge and free of books. Looking through the history books for various grades reveals a lot of unwanted and unrelated history being taught. All grade levels' textbook syllabuses must be revised on a regular basis to reflect the most recent updates.

In today's world, education is frequently obtained solely for the purpose of finding work. However, we must carefully consider the value of education. Education is essential for more than just getting a job. Education is one of the most important factors for a more dignified survival as well as the advancement of our society and nation. But, when we get a job or go about our daily lives, do we benefit from everything we learned in school and college? I'm fairly certain it's No. Then you must consider and analyse whether the current educational system needs to be changed or improved. We have made significant technological advances in the twenty-first century. Are we making progress as a species? Is it necessary to evolve in tandem with technological progress? Is it still necessary to learn new things in this case?.

Self-development should follow the advancement of technology in general. Skill-based learning is essential for self-development in today's world. Students should learn the necessary skills for success in this new world, then practise and apply them in their daily lives. The four C's should serve as the foundation for the main life skills: critical thinking, creativity, collaboration, and communication. To achieve the aforementioned objectives, parents' support and guidance are required. Parents may be unaware of all of these factors in their lives, and as a result, they may fail to raise their children with a positive attitude. Any child who focuses on these aspects will have a high chance of success in life.

When we talk about critical thinking, we mean analysing facts and information as well as critiquing claims. Creativity is the ability to think in novel ways and come up with novel ideas and solutions to problems. Understanding things well enough to clearly share them with others in the case of communication Collaboration is about teamwork and the collective genius of a group that is greater than the sum of its parts. Students, children, parents, and teachers must maintain positive relationships and understandings with one another throughout the educational process. Most of the time, the child does not understand the worth of many things, and parents are often unaware of many upgraded portions and their significance. Teachers, on the other hand, can use their influence to bring situations back into balance. Because their perspectives differ, the educational stage is critical for both the child and the parents. In this situation, parents should be very flexible, allowing the child to make decisions about his or her future while maintaining control over the child, offering advice as needed, and providing any necessary support. If things go in this direction, things at home can be very happy.

The Bhagavad Gita contains numerous lessons on education, particularly life skills. True wisdom teaches us to see God in all souls. The Lord declares that the supreme and essence of all pure knowledge were derived from a thorough study of the Vedas and various types of Upanishads. The importance of the soul is emphasised by Gita, and it is a secret part of knowledge: simply knowing that the pure soul is distinct from the body that will be destroyed. The soul remains unchanged and becomes immortal. It is constantly in use. To formulate educational principles, the divine teacher did not simply dictate his wisdom to his student. Gita explains the importance of such education. A human child is not an inanimate object in the world. From his previous life, he inherits certain tendencies, instincts, character traits, mental dispositions, and so on. The Gita reconciles metaphysics and physics, Nivruti and Pravrtti, psychical entities, and men's ancestry and environment, as well as educational principles that clearly show that education is a spiritual-social necessity. It is a value that cannot be founded on sand.

The teacher is determined to keep his student's soul and body intact, as well as his own. A student, rather than a disciple, is a learner, according to Gita. The concept of life skills is introduced here to demonstrate the significance of education. To begin, in order to progress in life, we must maintain a realistic and grounded perspective. To be successful, we must learn to be fighters, problem solvers, knowledge seekers, and, most importantly, risk takers. The Gita states that one must be a good communicator; everyone is familiar with Krishna's mischievous yet clever behaviour. He was skilled at persuading others and selling your ideas.

Gita has given much thought to mediation and its significance. Inner peace is achieved through mediation. Students' minds, which are always preoccupied with getting good grades, are unable to focus on mediation. When a student's mind is unstable and he thinks of success, it is a failed mediation attempt. According to Gita, the student must avoid three major vices in his personality: Kama, Krodha, and Lobha.

The following are the Bhagavad Gita's life skills education objectives:

1. Virtual knowledge creation
2. Personality growth and modification
3. Individual and social goals must be modified.
4. internal consciousness growth
5. Development of reasoning and intellectual abilities
6. Recognition of the importance of responsibilities in life

I am a firm believer that when we learn something, we must understand its worth and significance, as well as apply it to our own and others' development. The Bhagavad Gita emphasises the importance of education and living a good life in a proper manner, and all humans should follow suit. In that case, we can build a very good family, a very good society, and an excellent nation.

Our top priority should be to create a good family, society, and nation. Today's children, however, are unable to understand the value of anything because they are not taught about all of these topics. No one prioritises the importance of a good family, a good society, or the development of our country at home or in school. They will not make an effort to progress unless you inform them about all of these topics and generate interest in understanding their significance. As previously stated, education is now only used to obtain a job. You should reconsider these ideas, and you should put more emphasis on educating children about such issues.

A topic on family, society, and the nation should be included in the school curriculum, as well as the importance and need for each and every individual to contribute in some way to the development and creation of a beautiful nation. Every person should be proud to be a part of the country's progressive movement. Several methods are available. For example, if a boy is passionate about football, his talent should be nurtured, and the boy should understand that his participation and success in football can contribute to the development of a proud nation. It is critical to prioritise the creation of the country's name over obtaining a medal for the individual. Similarly, we are currently only concerned with ourselves in any field. Every child should be assigned a role in the development of our country and encouraged to participate in the process. Children should be encouraged to help the poor and needy from an early age. It must be physically practised so that the child develops a habit and recognises the importance of it. At a young age, children should understand the value of volunteering for charitable work. Every child should be delighted to share their once-a-day meal with someone who does not have access to a once-a-day meal. This type of action will keep children from becoming selfish and will encourage them to consider the poor and needy. If we can instil these characteristics in our children, they will almost certainly avoid bad habits because their minds have already generated sympathy.

Our country, and the world as a whole, is advancing technologically at a faster rate. Life became a lot easier after that. On the other hand, the value system and respect for people have completely vanished. Most of the young people have been instilled with Western culture and inhuman behaviour. In the eyes of children, anyone who tries to make them understand is a useless person. Children nowadays believe that they are the wisest, that they know far more than anyone else, and that they do not require any advice. With the same mindset, in our daily lives, parents and teachers have no role in developing children or recommending them for their upbringing. These situations exist solely as a result of new culture and technological advancement.

People are being led into a new world by adopting new cultures while forgetting our own culture and values. Even the elderly are benefiting from advancement, and as a result, they are able to adopt new culture, which they sometimes follow, and no one can blame them for losing value. If you create an atmosphere according to your own desires, it should not disturb anyone in the system. It should not have an impact on society or the country as a whole.

Chapter - 4

PARENTING

Parenting is a difficult task. However, whatever difficulties parents face in providing a bright future for their child and becoming a proud parent, they take it in stride. However, due to the so-called generation gap, children do not understand the difficulties or struggles of their parents and, in their opinion, it is the parents' responsibility and there is no need for gratitude. When they become a father or a mother, however, they will become selfish in order to care for their children. Even so, they will not value their own parents.

As a parent, you must have the vision of raising your child with proper guidance and setting many examples for a successful future by teaching values and respect, among other things. Even if the child makes a mistake, they do not mind and advise him or her quietly and without hurting the child, and with such treatment, the child will realise the mistake. On the other hand, if you start shouting for a simple mistake, the child will react and take it as revenge, repeating the mistake multiple times. As a parent, you are modelling good behaviour and provide sound advice to your children. However, I have seen many fathers and mothers yell at their children and make their children's lives miserable for trivial reasons. In such cases, the parents are immature and unconcerned about raising their child properly. In the other hand many children shouting at their parents and not respecting at all. When a child is below the age of 10 or 15, we can tolerate it and make the child understand. For simple reasons, many teenagers and even younger cause a lot of trouble for their parents. Breaking things at home, abusing parents, and making a mess of the house. Such cases must be taken seriously. In the event that there should be no excuses after doing everything for the child and ruining the parents' happiness. As previously stated, parenting is a difficult task. There are numerous sacrifices made in life to raise a child, such as providing a good education and taking care of everything. If the child does not understand the parents' difficulties and is bothering them and preventing them from having peace of mind, the child should be counselled to identify the problem. There are numerous cases where parents are at fault due to a lack of knowledge and a failure to focus on family matters, including the growth and education of their children. Such cases are to be treated as parental negligence. Whatever they experienced as children and witnessed from their parents is being passed on to the child, and children from such homes will undoubtedly not grow properly.

However, we can see many children from such homes learning well, behaving well, and progressing in life and reaching higher positions. As a result, children's development can be tailored to their specific needs and progressed accordingly. There are currently no institutions that teach parenting. So parenting is a cycle, and whatever they learned from their parents or grandparents, they will undoubtedly follow as it has been registered in their minds. It will come out as their reactions, whether they are aware of it or not. That is why we say family history is so important in our lives. Especially for ladies, because keeping the house and managing it will be a lady's art at home, as well as her responsibility. So it's all up to the lady at home. If she is educated and patient enough to handle the situation calmly, well matured the house will remain happy always. If she is always yelling and behaving with immature attitude, the house will never be happy.

As I have always believed and loved in my life, the lady at home is the lamp at home because she illuminates the entire home with a pleasant and lovable atmosphere. She is concerned about children and their proper education or growth. The man at home may be in charge of managing finances and other external responsibilities.

The mother's hands will be the first to shape the child's character and behaviour. She only teaches the child the value system. If the mother encourages lying, the child will follow suit. If a mother does not instil the value of a father in the mind of her child, the child will begin to disrespect the father. I have come across many parents, specially mother, who are lying about their children's grades. If a child earns 60%, the parent will tell others that the child earned 80%. It is actually a detriment to the child's overall attitude and will have an impact on the child's character development throughout his or her life. In such a case, the parent feels proud when mentioning the higher grades. Such small habits of parents are causing harm to the nation as a whole, not just the family. One should be grounded in reality. If the parent discloses the child's actual marks, the child will undoubtedly start thinking about getting more and taking pride in himself.

Value system is very important in our life. There is a space each and every members of the family and that should be respected. In many families, wives dominate their husbands and become involved in everything and anything, ignoring the value system. As the head of the family at home, a male member should be considered the first person at home. Everywhere in our ecosystem, whether it is an office or any organisation, there is a boss. As a custom and tradition, we respect it. If we require assistance, we immediately approach the boss, who will be given space and respect. As in the home, one leader is required to manage, and he or she should be the family's head.

To develop a strong and cohesive team, all other members must always respect his or her advice and directions. We focused on values and respect in Indian culture and in our ecosystem. It has meaning in life, and we must continue to do so, regardless of the generations. To restore the lost ecosystem of discipline required for a human being, parents must be more educative and understanding, as well as focused on training their children on the right path. If your children learn good things in life and begin to behave like a good human being, that will be the most important education and grade for them. In this world, marks don't mean much.

A child should be gifted, talented, and disciplined. The young generation now lives in a different culture influenced by Western style. To cope with the current system and culture, children should be involved in more activities that provide mental and physical strength, as well as opportunities to understand values and respect. One critical area is for the parent to understand the child's development in real time.

It is obvious that as children grow, their mental and physical activities will change, and this is a critical time to manage, especially during the adolescent years. Anticipating the challenges, parents should engage their children in various activities well before the same stage arrives, so that the activities can be continued alongside their studies. If the parents begin to think about the child and are unable to manage during the adolescent years, and plan to engage the child, it will cause severe problems for both the child and the parents.

When a child's mind and body develop the teenage syndrome he or she may divert their attention to various activities such as beginning to use various drugs and alcohol, as well as disrespecting parents when they resist anything or even their advice. Keeping children away from such activities at this time would be extremely dangerous. As a result, parents should spend time with their children on a daily basis to work with children to teach them values and respect, among other things. A child must understand his or her parents' capabilities in all areas. Children should rely on their parents only until a certain age, at which point they should become self-sufficient, for which he or she should devise a plan for earning money

Children are overprotected in this technological age, and they are so engrossed with various gadgets that they rarely have time for anything else.

The 5 C's are very important for a child's development, in my opinion.

Confidence, Compliments, Comparisons, Creative and Character. The development of a child's confidence is critical, and parents should praise their children for even the smallest accomplishments.

Complimenting will encourage the child to do better things one by one. This will also help the child's brain development. Always encourage your child to engage in creative activities. It will help his brain develop faster and faster.

Character development is critical, and the mother's involvement is crucial. A child is only closely attached to his or her mother, and any advice given to the child by the mother is considered appropriate. All these development can be part of their education.

Chapter - 5

ROLL OF A TEACHER

What does the Bhagavad Gita have to say about teachers?

Lord Chaitanya stated that a teacher should be properly behaved even before beginning to teach. One who teaches in this manner is known as acharya, or the ideal teacher. To reach the common man, a teacher must adhere to the principles of sastra (scripture).

It is undeniable that technology has facilitated new learning while also altering the course of education. A good teacher, on the other hand, has the power to change our lives and ignite us in the most perfect way. A teacher is an important part of our lives. Every year on September 5th, India celebrates Teacher's Day to show respect and gratitude to all teachers in the country. The birthday of Dr Sarvepally Radhakrishnan, the second president of our country is being celebrated in our country as Teachers day. He was a great philosopher and statesman. He was the first vice president of India for continuously for two terms before he becoming the 2nd President of India. He was the 4th vice chancellor of Banaras Hindu University and 2nd vice chancellor of Andhra University. Dr Sarvepally Radhakrishnan's belief that "teachers should be the best minds in the country"

Dr APJ Abdul Kalam writes that if people remember me as good teacher it will be the biggest honour for me.

Teachers play an important role in a child's development from the moment he or she begins learning with the teacher, whether in pre-primary, primary, or any grade. After parents, teachers are the most important people in everyone's lives.

According to our former President, late Dr Abdul Kalam, teaching is a very noble profession that shapes an individual's character, calibre, and future. The greatest honour for me will be if people remember me as a good teacher. Every educated person cannot become a teacher. People who choose the profession of teaching do so with zeal. Teaching is an art that can only be practised with a certain amount of discipline. Teachers must serve as role models not only in educational institutions but also in society. Teachers have a different value and respect in society because they are the main pillar for the development of future leaders. As I mentioned earlier, I always consider the four entities in life is **Matha, Pitha, Guru, and Daivam.** All of these things are crucial in life, and teachers are no exception.

A good teacher will be a student's friend, and the teacher will clearly know the child. Some teachers will know more about the child than his or her parents. Teachers must maintain a close relationship with the child and must be sympathetic and lovable. Teaching is a noble profession, and children and society will regard a teacher based on his or her dealings and knowledge.

A good teacher will always be encouraging to both the parent and the student. A teacher is the most remembered person on the planet. How many children does a teacher have to teach over the course of their career, and how many of those children graduate? As a result, a teacher must have certain qualities, such as:

A teacher must be well-informed.

A teacher should be courteous and sympathetic.

A teacher should be extremely helpful to both students and parents.

A teacher should be a role model in every way.

A teacher must be punctual and disciplined.

A teacher must be well-organized.

A teacher should be a good leader too.

In the school, a teacher should play the role of a father or mother.

Learning is an ongoing process that occurs every day. We learn things in our lives from a variety of sources, and there is always a teacher or mentor involved. So a teacher plays an important role, and no matter what the numbers are, one cannot forget his or her teacher.

One should emulate Bill. Bill Campbell is a former football coach turned entrepreneur. He rose to international prominence as a result of his ability to coach CEOs of major corporations such as Google and Apple. It is well known that Bill Campbell was one of the most integral to Google's success, and the company would not be where it is today without him. He was coaching various CEOs while working with Google's senior team and with Steve Jobs at Apple. He coached many CEOs and many other personalities like Brad Smith, former Intuit CEO, John Donahoe, former eBay CEO, US Vice President AL Gore, Dick Costolo, former Twitter CEO, Mike McCue, CEO of Flipboard, Donna Dubinsky, CEO of Numentra, Nirav Tolia, CEO of Nextdoor, Lee C Bollinger, President of Columbia University, Shellye Archambeau, former CEO of MetricStream, Ben Horowitz, partner at venture capital firm Andreessen Horowitz, Boys and girls flag footballs teams at Sacred Heart, Bill Gurley, general partner at venture capital firm Benchmark. NFL Hall of Famer Ronnie Lott, Danny Shader, CEO of Handle Financial, Sundar Pichai, CEO of Google, Dan Rosenzweig, CEO of Chegg, Charlie Batch, fellow Homestead native and former quarterback for the Pittsburgh Stealer's, Jesse Rogers, managing director of Altamont Capital Partners, John Hennessy, former president of Stanford University, Sheryl Sandberg, COO of face book.

According to the analysis, Bill Campbell's transition from football coach, caddie, and CEO coaching many personalities will be a great one. The knowledge he shared with others aided the company's growth. That is the impact of a teacher, mentor, or coach. A teacher is someone who deserves a lot of respect in our lives. However, in today's world, how many of us respect our teachers?

You can do great things for society as a teacher. A teacher creates and develops various professionals in our country, and without them, nothing moves. All development in our country is the result of the teachers' community effectively sharing knowledge on various subjects by teaching the subject and making the students rich with knowledge shower.

When a teacher does a great job of developing future leaders and various professionals such as scientists, doctors, engineers, police officers, army officers, and IAS officers, among others, are we remembering the effort of a teacher who makes a genuine effort to help students study and advance to the next division? A teacher must remember his or her students throughout his or her life. Similarly, a student should remember his or her teacher throughout his or her life, regardless of position. Your position and power are solely due to your teachers' efforts and your parents' support. So don't forget about your teachers. Remember and respect them, listen to them, and value them, and you will be blessed.

Chapter - 6

BEHAVIOUR OF CHILDREN TOWARDS PARENTS

A child should learn to respect his or her parents because they are the manifestation of God on this planet in whom we believe. It is the child's responsibility to respect the parents, whether they have faults or not. Parents will always support, love, and protect their children. When they appear to be very strict, it is only to protect us from potential harm. As a child, you should appreciate your parents' efforts and show some respect for them.

A child should listen to them and obey whatever they say. Acceptance and respect are the best mantras for parents. A child who respects and accepts his or her parents will undoubtedly be blessed. During the journey of education a child should learn all these from the surroundings, even if no one teach them on these aspects. Parents blessing are the biggest achievement in life.

Children are tomorrow's leaders. They build a good family, a good society, and a good nation. they can create a beautiful country if they focus on the importance of all of these? When I think back on my childhood, I remember how important values and respect were. In a joint family, the decision maker was the family's head, and everyone used to obey happily and without hesitation.

Everyone was treated with dignity and respect regardless of their age. Everyone adored one another. Mutual love, affections, value, and respect are all now on paper, and nobody gives them any weight these days. Who creates new stages of life? All our beautiful cultures are being faded away. The only reason for these changes is the young generation's attitude and thought process.

A child who obeys his or her parents and elders will succeed if they work hard enough. However, the majority of today's youth are well educated and acting as if they have reached the pinnacle of their lives and can do anything and everything without the support of their parents. They forget to respect their parents during the same process. They are becoming selfish and living their own lives. They have no recollection of their parents' efforts to get them to this point.

A mother who is only concerned with her children's well-being. She was familiar with their eating habits and preferences. She is intimately acquainted with their children. She prepares food to their liking and serves it with love. Mothers frequently forget to eat because their primary concern is feeding their children. Throughout her life, she will only think about their children, whether they become senior citizens or otherwise. Having done all of this, many children who have reached the age of taking on family responsibilities are abusing, hitting, and harassing their mother like a dog, possibly under the influence of alcohol or drugs.

Mother is only becoming the victim, and a violent children will not attack their father because they are afraid. However, they take unfair advantage of their mother, and she is the only one who suffers as a result. Despite her pain, she will not reveal it to anyone, including her husband, most of the time. Such children cannot be referred to as children in this contest, they are adults.

A mother always stands by us in good and bad times. For the mother, their children are exact. She always looks after and loves us more than anyone else in her life. We don't exist unless Mother is present.

Mother is a precious word, and she is the foundation of our lives. Mothers must be protected, loved, and respected. It is extremely difficult to live without a mother. Even at any age, the presence of a mother provides energy and a different vibration in our daily lives. This is thinking about who is a more significant angle between the Mother and a God, and it falls into the larger conscience.

Mother is referred to as Amma, Mom, Mummy, Maa and other variations. We must call her whatever we want. A person who does not value, respect, love, and affectionately towards his or her mother will not succeed in life, no matter how hard they work.

Amma or Maa is the first word a child ever says. When a child is worried or scared about something, the first thing that comes to mind is my maa. Whatever success or happiness we have, we tell our mother first, and similarly, we tell our mother first about our worries and difficulties. Because there is a power in the universe that is unseen, magical, and greater than any God in this world.

Child and mother affection is not only in human beings, but it also deeply seen in animals and birds too. Animals and birds are superior to humans if we pay close attention to them. Sometimes we need to learn the bonding of father, mother, and children from these categories.

Everything is so advanced in the new technological era, and people's priorities have shifted dramatically. In this scenario, mothers who are not well educated are neglected by their children under the guise of her inability in various aspects of life. She might not look good, not having good manners, or do not know how to behave well.

Many children nowadays disrespect their parents by making fun of them, yelling at them, and blaming them for ridiculous reasons. They consider themselves to be an encyclopaedia and a knowledge bank. Such children regard their parents as worthless. However, parents should meet all of their obligations right away. Many children, both boys and girls, become addicted to alcohol and drugs and lead a different lifestyle. They are beyond the parents' or anyone's control. They believe that whatever they do is correct and continue to live in their own world. However, after a few years, they will undoubtedly repent of their actions. Those who disregard their parents' advice and fail to respect the rules will lose their beautiful lives. Many children, particularly those from low-income or middle-class families who have struggled for a living, will respect their parents, and such children will respect everyone as a human being. Such children will appreciate everything and view life as a challenge. They will provide a good life for their parents considering their effort and hard work put in to grow them. In life, good behaviour is extremely important. In life, one should learn to be very humble and decent. It is critical to respect elders and to value everything. Some children who were raised with all value systems change their patterns when they reach the adolescent stage due to the influence of their peers.

A girl child who experiences all stages of life quickly, including adolescence, and who becomes a mother at a young age. Carrying a child in her stomach and adding to her difficulties throughout her life. In this world, the visible god is a mother. Her love and affection are unavailable anywhere in the world, and there is no substitute for a mother. As we all know, the stepmother will not provide adequate love and affection. So each of us pledges to love our mother, respect our mother more than anything else on the planet, care for her until her death, and to remember her even after her death till your last breath.

Those who have mothers right now are fortunate to have their mothers' love and affection.

I lost both my parents a long time ago, and I still miss them. In my case, they were unable to provide anything, and I was unable to enjoy their love, affection, and pampering because they were constantly stressed due to financial constraints. I had them before I started my career. If they had been with me, I would have taken good care of them and kept them happy. But I missed it....and wished for a second chance to stay with my mother and father and care for them.

Love your mother, respect her, look after her and protect her. Give her peace of mind and she needs your love and affection only, nothing else. Do not hurt her in your life, if so it will be a curse on you automatically and unknowingly. According to Veda, the feminine is the mother of gods, the womb of cosmic creation. Because the living deity is housed in a temple's sacred-womb space known as the garbha griha, the temple is regarded as the mother herself, the pristine source of highest life-energy. The entire motherhood is elevated as a divine principle in Vedic culture; not only is the mother considered sacred. The life-giving maternal power is repeatedly praised in the ancient Vedas, where everything sacred, pure, and powerful is elevated to the status of a mother. Aditi, the mother of devas, emperors, and sages, Sarasvati, the goddess of celestial waters, Ushas, the dawn mother, and Prithvi, the earth mother are some of her many names..

If you look for the value of mother in any form, you will be amazed that mother is everything. Why do we refer to our country as Mother India, with the utmost respect? So we should all touch our mothers' feet once a day to show her our love and respect. Everything revolves around Mother. Mother is the sole provider. Mother is a relation unlike all. Our consciousness and every other relation originates from our mother. A woman is not the object of a man's desire, but she is the mother, the maker, the provider and keeper, and the leader. The mother in every woman commands our soulful affection and care, as there is none greater to mother on earth.

With all due respect, any person, who disrespects or harms his or her mother will face serious consequences in life. There are no corrective measures.

Similarly, our father, who is the most responsible person at home, will take care of everything, including our education and other needs. The importance of hard work and dedication to the family and family members' well-being cannot be overstated. A father as a person has no room to relax or express his feelings because he cannot reveal his concerns while others are happy. He moves forward with everything in his heart. Generally, fathers are role models for children; however, the demands of children on various aspects are making him concerned, and if he fails to complete or does not accept the viewpoint of children, he is a useless father.

In our society, there are clearly many good children and adults who live solely for their parents. I sincerely appreciate them all and hold them in high regard. They are the only true humans on the planet. They are the most successful person in their lives. They will be respected in society and will be blessed.

Everything, as I have always believed, is our creation. Those who can think logically create a happy family, a happy society, and a happy nation. We have complete control over everything. God created us to do our own creations, which allow you to enjoy your life for generations to come. Your thought process will only help you live a happy life. Your happiness will spread throughout the world, causing many positive things to happen for the best, and you will be recognised at the same time. Your exceptional efforts to help others and society will be recognised, and you will be regarded as a good human being in the eyes of others.

Chapter - 7

HUSBAND, WIFE AND THEIR BEHAVIOUR

Marriage is an essential component of our lives and the life cycle. Bringing two people together and becoming life partners for life with the blessings of parents and loved ones. This story brings together two minds, two bodies, two hearts, two thoughts, two dreams, two visions, two opinions, two ideas, and two souls. Trying to live as a single heart, soul, and mind. Adjusting two minds and bodies in one's life will result in complete satisfaction, limitless happiness, and a sense of security, support, and protection for everything.

According to Veda, marriage is a union between a masculine and feminine entity with commitments to pursue Dharma (duty), Artha (earning money and other possessions), Kama physical and other desires) and Moksha (the eternal liberation) in unison.

If we think about ladies, leaving their own home and adjusting to a new member of a new family, a new person as a husband with a lot of responsibilities on her shoulders. Two unknown person getting together in a sudden moment. The newly wedded wife will be completely unsure of what to do and how to do it because everyone in her new home will be watching her, or she must believe that everyone will be watching her through her actions and words. However, She will adjust to the new circumstances as quickly as possible. She must play the roles of a responsible wife, a wonderful daughter-in-law, a sister-in-law, and many others. She must develop courage and acceptance of the new situation in order to adjust to it. It was a new adventure and the beginning of a new life for her. She will be completely dependent on her husband. If her husband does not support her at that stage, she may fail to perform, become concerned, and curse the new circumstances. The husband, the new person in her life, will show her enough love through his physical and mental presence. However, understanding her in the right form, particularly her feelings, recognising, and supporting her will be a significant role for him. The initial actions should be a memorable time in her lifetime. So begins a pleasant and happy life.

On the other hand, the wife plays an important role in her husband's life. Understanding his routine, likes, passions, priorities, visions, discipline, mind, worries, food habits, clothing choices, concern for his parents and siblings, and so on is critical. Understanding him and responding based on that would be a basic requirement as a partner, and it would also help to draw his complete love.

The fundamental understanding developed by the newlywed husband and wife will serve as a foundation for the rest of their lives. At this point, they can assess their life's happiness and sorrow and easily understand how they drive their life. Mutual understanding is extremely important.

The most significant trend in this era is divorce shortly after marriage. Today they are married, and tomorrow they will be divorced. In that case, why are they carrying out the marriage ceremony, which requires extensive planning, effort, and financial investment? It can be supported if both couples are unable to continue their relationship in the young age itself. Divorce should be done before having a child or at a younger age.

A married life is mutual understanding and situation management for the sake of success and happiness. Male and female partners will exist in all living things, whether birds, animals, or plants. Without it, there will be no further development of the community. As a result, the system exists not only in humans but in all living things. But, with this partnership game, we have complete control over how we live our lives.

We have three important stages in our lives as humans. These are: young, middle, and old. Marriages will occur at a young age, and many transformations or developments will happen, such as childbirth, child education, child settlement, buying or constructing a house, buying a car and many more.

All of this will happen thanks to the efforts of both husband and wife. Having a happy and successful family with blessed children is only possible if you work hard for it with a human touch. As I previously stated, counting the grades of children, the parents will reach old age. From young age to middle age, we can take on and fulfil responsibilities, and in old age, we should have peace of mind, adequate rest, and happiness.

But the question is, how many people live happy lives? Why do some people have fulfilling relationships while others fail? Are we on the right track? There are numerous reasons for this.

A life begins with the couple, the husband and wife, and it is their responsibility to plan for a good life. How many of us make a firm plan for our lives from young age to old age? In the meantime, we must overcome numerous obstacles, ups and downs, progress or achievements, various pleasures, numerous setbacks, and accumulating growth, among other things. Are all of these events going as planned? It happens based on the situations and needs we have at the time. But, from the start of our marriage, we should devise a strategy for increasing our success. A planned life will only bring you success, and with that, we begin to focus on our goal.

Due to various requirements in life as well as numerous challenges, a difference of opinion or dislike will develop between the couple, or so-called husband and wife, through their life's journey.

It can cause people anxiety, tension, and depression. Once a disagreement begins, it will occur frequently and cause complications. They begin to forget the love and affection they were sharing. In many cases, the opening between the husband and wife will begin later in life, by which time their children will have grown up and it will be time to marry and settle down.

In many cases, the disagreement will begin at the beginning, and they will be able to make a firm decision to continue or not continue their life together or plan for separation through a divorce.

If two people are unable to reconcile at such a young age, the best option is to seek legal separation. However, you cannot continue to wish for a better life because the next partner may be worse than the previous one. As a result, one should not have the impression that the other side's green is good.

In many cases, the initial difference of opinion has been about managing and continuing life as usual with little fight in between, moving to depression at times, concern for the children, family, and society, and so on. However, if the conflict escalates and they decide to divorce in middle age, by the time their children are grown up and ready to get married and settle, it will be disastrous for their children.

In our society, no one considers a second marriage while their spouse is still alive. In the event of one's death, it may be considered for support for the rest of one's life. So, separating through divorce and planning to live alone in middle age will have lot of in security. Nobody will have the happy and pleasant life that we expect.

Life is all about making changes. If someone can adjust his or her life for the sake of children and their education, or for a variety of other reasons, for a long time, why can't they do the same for the rest of their lives? Instead, it will help the children have a bright future.

No husband and wife should plan to divorce after they reach middle age, when their children are about to settle down. That is the time for them to speak up and move forward with more conviction and courage. They can satisfy their children while maintaining their social standing if they are unhappy. Divorce has an impact on society, and many people begin to criticise it in various ways. A woman who is divorced and living in society is unable to live a decent life. She will be neither safe nor secure. Society will mark her in a deplorable manner. Even if she believes she is healthy and strong, she will require care and support at some point. Because she is alone in such cases, the people around her may not provide complete support. There will be widespread fear among the populace. Instead, people start taking advantage of her or troubling her in many ways. Even if she is a perfect woman, she will not be safe and will have to face numerous problems.

In the case of a male member, there will be no issues, and he will receive a great deal of support from those around him. He will not lose his image because his surroundings may not care why he lives alone. On the other hand, a woman living alone or with children after divorce will face increased criticism and will undoubtedly lose her perception of how simple life can be.

You need to start believing that your previous life was far superior to your current one. A lady will be respected in the family and society as long as she spends her time with her parents, husband, and children. Even if your children do not behave well, you can find enjoyment in life only with your spouse and children.

In my opinion, our children are the future leaders. Whatever disagreements the couple has should not have an impact on the physical and moral strength of our children. Why did you prepare for marriage if you can't bear the burden and accept adversity? So, in order to grow as an individual and for society as a whole, life should not be taken lightly, and you should embrace all challenges. It is the outcome of our efforts. Make a strong bond, a strong mind, and a good life with your current situation to ensure success. Our actions must all set a good example. Many people in society will attempt to lead you astray. You must make your own decision and act as your own judge.

Creating a happy family is an art that requires a lot of patience and strength. Everyone in the family should work together to make their home a happy and progressive place. If we do this, there will be no conflict in the family, whether between husband and wife or between children. People's opinions will differ, and this is a necessary part of our survival and progress. Progress will occur when the valid point is accepted without ego. Conflicts occur when no one accepts the point as valid. We frequently associate with our friends, family members, and members of various organisations in our daily lives. We are able to maintain a stable and fair relationship with them. Why are we creating such a situation within our home when we will not begin to hold grudges with people outside? Do not dig your own grave; adjustments will give you space, which will lead to happiness and success. Making a happy family is the stability you are creating in your life, and this action should be an example for many others.

When a person decides to divorce because of a failure in his or her current life, he or she must have chosen someone for his or her life, and this must be the motivation. As a result, the escapism from the current burden includes forgetting about his or her children's future. When a family is disrupted, the innocent children suffer the most. Their adored parents left an indelible imprint on their children's lives for the rest of their lives.

The main reason for deciding to divorce is comparison; when you see other happy couples, you will notice many qualities in them. However, if you interact with them closely, you will realise that you or your spouse are good. Can anyone get rid of your parents for any reason? The answer is emphatically no. Similarly, if you have been together for longer than the time you have been with your parents for whatever reason, how can you decide to divorce? According to religious books such as the Bible or the Quran, God does not support divorce. Any problems can be solved through commitments and discussions. It could happen several times, and you might change your mind concerning your ownership. You'll be successful.

According to a recent survey, the most common reason given by divorcing couples is a lack of commitment. The following are the reasons given, along with their percentages: 73% lacked commitment, while 56% argued excessively.

So you are the creator of everything, and you are solely responsible for your life. All of this happens as a result of your thought process or negativity within you as you wish for a better life. However, there may be circumstances beyond our control, such as when you are neglected or your contributions to the family are not recognised. Even so, keep in mind that these are your own people, and they can only play with you. If you keep your mind at that level, everything in life is manageable. We cannot hate anyone, particularly our own people, but we can keep people away from us in order to avoid making aggressive decisions. The marriage relationship states that once you enter someone's life, you must stay with him or her until your last breath. Do not believe that the greens on the other side are good.

There is no good life after you have been divorced from your surviving spouse. Children who are close to you or who recommend your separation will not help you later, and they will also detach from you if you are the father or mother.

We must set an example in our lives, and you must satisfy yourself. Your spouse, kids, and other members of society occasionally dislike the good deeds you do. Let it be; your satisfaction is the most important certification. There are many difficulties in our lives. Even if you have problems and are dissatisfied with your marriage, you should stick with it until your last breath. Consider it your success in life.

That would be the completion of your creation. We are the ones who create everything. Everything is in our hands, whether we do good or bad, whether we succeed or fail, whether we advance or fall, whether we have a happy or broken family. Do good for your family, do good for society, and do great nation-building.

It is our creation, as I have stated several times. Everything, including your success, failure, happiness, and sorrow, is in your hands. Nobody is to blame for this. You should all strive to build a good family, society, and nation. Put in the effort. One of the factors influencing our actions will be our behavioural patterns. If every individual, whether young, middle-aged, or elderly, including children, parents, and teachers, decided to do well in life with their creations, all of our actions would produce very positive results, culminating in a very pleasant atmosphere wherever we are. Everyone is responsible for contributing to the success and happiness of the family. Your family is yours alone, and you are possessive of it.

Those who respect their "Matha," "Pitha," "Guru," and "Daivam" (mother, father, teacher, and god) are said to live long, happy lives and improve the world for their future generations. Your parents are your gods in the flesh, so treat them with respect. You will get nowhere without their help, but if you have enough respect for them, you can go a long way.

That's all about fulfilment in your creation. Your creations should be successful; do not give them a chance for failure.

Chapter - 8

CREATING A GOOD SOCIETY

We are all members of a community and share responsibility for its development. The people who live in a society that is well-run will reap many rewards. The work put into making a community safe and secure pays dividends for years to come. We can't make it without the support of other humans; we need each other to live. Neighbours today rarely talk to one another and often don't even know each other's names. Everyone has become insular and focused solely on themselves.

Everyone benefits from and thrives in a flourishing community. A healthy community provides the foundation for education at all ages. Confidence and bravery are bolstered through contact with people of all ages in society. Children benefit academically and socially from the many celebrations, parties, and other events that adults organise for them throughout the year. As we get to know one another in a variety of settings, we begin to view one another as members of the same family. There is an immediate need for people to treat each other with respect and cooperate with one another through both positive and negative experiences.

When you have compassion for someone else's plight, you have an obligation to publicly show your support without being asked. Regarding one's network of support, one must avoid becoming self-centred. As a community, we have incredible potential to foster growth and elevate its members.

Every day, people should work towards creating an ideal society. Every household has an obligation to serve as an example for others in the community. It's important that everyone present participate in whatever is going on. Water conservation, efficient home electricity use, community safety, and so on should all be part of larger community-wide awareness campaigns. Communities also need to take care of the environment by doing things like planting trees and keeping trash to a minimum. Separate gatherings could be held for a variety of causes, including environmental protection, charity work, mutual benefit programmes, and mentoring for advanced students.

Every group has a voice in any given society, and it's important to listen to what they have to say.

Every member of every society needs access to basic biographical information so they can quickly and easily identify anyone else. Everyone, regardless of social standing, should pitch in at least once every three months to clean up the community. Our kids can learn a lot from these types of experiences, so we need to include them in the team as much as possible. There are a variety of ways that the children can learn when we engage in such activities.

ABOUT THE AUTHOR

The author is a former military officer. He has a doctorate in human rights and serves as National Vice President of the World Human Rights Protection Commission on the national level in addition to being a permanent member on the international level. He was named best author of 2022 for his book, The Journey Through Life in Search of Success, which was released in November of that year. On September 9, 2022, he was honoured with the Indian Icon Award for his tireless advocacy on behalf of cancer patients. He triumphed over the disease despite overwhelming odds.

He is an extremely diligent person whose efforts and self-discipline have paid off handsomely. Since he was a youngster, he has faced adversity, but by taking risks, he has ultimately prevailed. He has compassion for everyone he meets and is a selfless benefactor.